a day in
ROCKPORT
Massachusetts

Scenes from a Coastal Town

The Paper Mermaid Press

For Mattie: my rock and safe harbor.
~ M. F.

To everyone who loves the little town of Rockport, having spent a day (or many) in this lovely place.
~ S. D. K.

Pictures © by Mary Faino
Words © by S.D. Kelly
All Rights Reserved

ISBN 978-1-7322085-3-7
First Edition, June 2015
Published by **The Paper Mermaid, LLC**
57 Main Street, Rockport, MA 01966

www.papermermaid.com

a day in ROCKPORT

Pictures by
Mary Faino

Words by
S.D. Kelly

A boat heads out
in the quiet morning hours –
the hours between the stars
and the sun.

A small still pond
in a green, green meadow.

The turtle says good morning,
the frog says good night,
just before the sun comes up.

The headstones lean this way.
The headstones lean that way.

The light warms the rock
and the rock warms the cat.
The cat watches the sea below
in the early morning sun.

There's a party at
the Old Sloop Church.
Friends and flowers fill the lawn,
banners flutter in the breeze,

under the light of the noonday sun.

The old gallery is big and bright.
Curious eyes pry and want to know
of men and mermaids and quarries and boats.

The artists don't say much
but their pictures do, tucked here,
out of the midday sun.

Time for a walk along the street
where bright shops line both sides,
all the way to the end, all the way to the sea.

Stop for some ice cream.
Eat it fast before it melts
in the heat of the afternoon sun.

The little boats sail out of the harbor and into open water.
Soft rain passes overhead.

It's time to come home now.
Skies clear and make way
for the light of the late day sun.

Set up the easel
when the light is just right.
Sketch the old red fishing shack
still on the wharf:
a little bit different,
but mostly the same.

Beyond the wharf, the ocean glows,
reflecting the evening sun.

The boats are all home now
just inside the breakwater,
inside the light of the setting sun.

The tired cat curls up to nap
on the crisscross of a lobster trap.
Lights twinkle overhead.
The time has come to say
good night.

Rockport, Massachusetts
Originally an outpost of Gloucester, Rockport was first settled in 1623, and incorporated in 1840. Featured in this book are just a few of the sites that make it such a special place.

Millbrook Meadow   *pp. 8-9*
The second settler in Sandy Bay, John Pool, created the Mill Pond to supply water power for his grist mill in 1702. The pond and adjacent meadow have been preserved from development for the enjoyment of Rockport residents and visitors (including birds, frogs and turtles).

Front Beach   *pp. 10-11*
Front Beach is a curved, sandy beach right in the heart of Rockport, where generations of Rockport children have learned to swim -- and picked up sea glass and other treasures.

Old First Parish Burial Ground   *pp. 12-13*
Rockport's first cemetery dates to 1640 and is the burial site of most of Rockport's first settlers. It is situated on a lovely slope overlooking the ocean; its ancient slate headstones offer a glimpse into another time.

Old Sloop Church   *pp. 14-15*
Originally a colonial meeting house, the First Congregationalist Church was nicknamed "The Old Sloop" by fisherman in the early 1800s. The church steeple was shot by the crew of a British frigate during the War of 1812. The church still has the cannonball.

Rockport Art Association & Museum   *pp. 16-17*
Located in an old sea captain's house, the Rockport Art Association & Museum (RAA&M) was

founded in 1921 by artists as a cooperative for showing and selling their work. Many decades later, the RAA&M is still a vibrant organization, with over 250 artist-members and a long history as the center of Rockport's community of artists and art-lovers.

Bearskin Neck   *pp. 18-19*
Bearskin Neck is made up of a few streets at the tip of Rockport lined with old fish shacks and sail lofts, relics of the fishing industry in earlier centuries, now used as homes, shops and galleries. The Neck is named after a legend in which a man named Ebenezer Babson killed a menacing bear with a fish knife, stretching the skin on the rocks to dry.

Straitsmouth Island   *p. 21*
Straitsmouth Island is jointly owned by the Massachusetts Audubon Society as a bird sanctuary and the Town of Rockport. The current Straitsmouth Light, the lighthouse on the island, was built in 1896 and is still in operation.

Rockport Harbor   *pp. 22-23*
The first dock was built in the harbor in 1743. Over the centuries, Rockport was the site for timber, fishing and granite industries. Today, lobstermen still dock alongside pleasure boats in Rockport's busy harbor.

Motif No. 1   *p. 22*
This red fishing shack on Bradley Wharf was originally built for fisherman to store and mend gear. It was so picturesque, artists of the early 20th century painted and sketched it repeatedly, leading one art teacher, Lester Hornby, to declare it "Motif No. 1". The original Motif blew down during the Blizzard of '78 and residents immediately rallied to build a replica, which still serves fishermen today as a working fish shack and artists from all over the world as a subject.

www.ingramcontent.com/pod-product-compliance
Lightning Source LLC
Chambersburg PA
CBHW041110070526
44583CB00003B/132